I0421686

Stress, Relaxation and Coloring Books

Peacefulness for Busy People

Dragana Dj. Jeremic

Dragana@relax8.space

https://relax8.space

Independent Publishing

Copyright © 2019 Dragana Dj. Jeremic.
All Rights Reserved.

No part of this publication may be reproduced, translated, distributed, or transmitted in any form or by any means, including photocopying, recording, or other electronic or mechanical methods, or by any information storage and retrieval system without the prior written permission of the author, except in the case of very brief quotations embodied in critical reviews and certain other noncommercial uses permitted by copyright law. It is illegal to copy this book, post it to a website, or distribute it by any other means without permission from the author.

Book design

Dragana Dj. Jeremic

Limits of Liability and Disclaimer of Warranty

The author and publisher shall not be liable for your misuse of this material. This book is strictly for informational and educational purposes.

Warning – Disclaimer

The purpose of this book is to educate and entertain. The author and/or publisher do not guarantee that anyone following these techniques, suggestions, tips, ideas, or strategies will become successful. The author and/or publisher shall have neither liability nor responsibility to anyone with respect to any loss or damage caused, or alleged to be caused, directly or indirectly by the information contained in this book.

Your Gift: Mini Workbook PDF

This convenient PDF file is the gift companion to Dragana's book *Stress, Relaxation and Coloring Books*. Here is the link for her Amazon author page: https://amazon.com/author/draganajoy The PDF has six paragraphs from Dragana's book and six related practices. Easy to use. Enjoy the book and the gift.

I am glad we may create the online relationship.
Here is the link for the gift. Please keep the link private.
https://relax8.space/peace1/

Review request

I appreciate that we spent time together engaging with "Stress, Relaxation and Coloring Books". If you found this book helpful, I would be grateful for your review.

Welcome to my Amazon author page

https://amazon.com/author/draganajoy

Find the title "Stress, Relaxation and Coloring Books", scroll down and click WRITE A CUSTOMER REVIEW button. Every vote is important. You may opt for stars only. Alternatively, another choice is writing one or several sentences to post the review.

Leaving a rating for Dragana's books on will help other people find this book. You'll also support an independent author Dragana by posting your review.

About the Author

Dragana Dj. Jeremic is a master psychologist, master jurist, photographer and English instructor among other hats she is keen on wearing as a life-long learner as well as spiritual seeker.
She became the Certified HeartMath Practitioner in 2024, after exploringHearhMath technics for several years.

https://certified.heartmath.com/user/dragana-jeremic/

Here is *the Summer Challenge 2024 Catalogue* link where you may enjoy 43 images including Dragana's on page 7.

https://issuu.com/digweb/docs/solstice_v2

Table of Contents

1) Introduction

Relaxation is important. Do you know why?

In this short read we will explore stress, relaxation and relaxing aspects of coloring books. Many people forget or underestimate these topics. If they knew why the subjects were important to them, they would make different choices and behaviors. Therefore, I wrote this book.

Coloring books are popular. It is easy to take an approach of an extremist. Certain groups may underestimate them as one of the relaxation techniques. Or "colorists" may idealize the coloring. We will contemplate limitations and benefits of coloring books.

What are coloring books? Each person may express they unique perspective on coloring books. "The only artistic skill you need is the ability to hold a colored pencil or a marker between your fingers and fill in a space," ("Art therapy Coloring", n. d., para. 2). However, what are the common elements? Each coloring book contains line art, while drawings are available in various formats, themes and complexity. In short, the fans color between the lines using artistic media such as colored pencils, crayons or paint. Coloring utensils are available online, too.

The structure of this book allows the reader to appreciate the author's ideas. In addition, Dragana dedicated every other chapter to ideas of other authors. She summarized online articles on the topics in this book in one paragraph, which has made it easier to appreciate different perspectives on stress, relaxation and relaxing aspects of coloring books. Reference section at the end of this book contains links and data, so you may study further the online articles.

Which one of the three subjects you prefer?

First, Dragana invites you to think about stress and our ability to manage it. What are consequences of disregarded stress?

Second, we contemplate the relaxation; we explore its benefits.

Third, what are the relaxing aspects of coloring books? Is it easy to appreciate them? You are in control with the coloring. The author of this book considers the benefits of coloring and acknowledges their limitations. So, you may choose what suits you the best.

Dragana Dj. Jeremic will release her first coloring book soon. People who have seen the drawings notice an abstract quality to the images, even that the drawings resemble to Dali's style of artistic expression.

2) Summary of Three Online Articles on Stress

In this chapter we contemplate three perspectives on stress expressed in online articles. We need to know facts on stress to relieve it better. In addition, it helps us to gain a wider perspective on the subject when we appreciate points of view of different authorities.

In "Understanding and Managing Stressors" Elizabeth Scott", MS (2018, Oct 30) explains the difference between the stressors and the stress. Sometimes people use those words as synonyms, but they have a distinct meaning. Scott supports that a stressor is an event we perceive as a dangerous or demanding factor, while stress is the effect of the stressor on us. Do stressors have universal meaning for each human being? Scott argues, "Stressors are situations experienced as a perceived threat to one's well-being or position in life, when the challenge of dealing with which, exceeds the person's perceived available resources," (Scott, 2018, Oct 30, para. 1). She notes how the same event may produce various effects on people. When you spend time in a shopping mall, is it a stressor? Scott points out for one person it may be a dangerous position, for another is a non-significant daily task, while the experience may delight the third person.

Scott concludes that the subjective nature of the potential stressors gives us power to manage stress.

According to "The Effects of Stress on Your Body" (WebMD Medical Reference) (2017, Dec 10) stress has various aspects. What is stress? What types of stress are possible? From what direction may you expect the stress? "Stress is any change in the environment that requires your body to react and adjust in response. The body reacts to these changes with physical, mental, and emotional responses," (WebMD Medical Reference, 2017, Dec 10, para. 1). The article argues although stress is a regular part of life, it is not the one and only stress. We differentiate the desirable stress "eustress" from the undesirable stress "distress". The article further states we often refer to distress, and how to minimize the stress or avoid it. The article provides information on the consequences of disregarded distress whether it comes from the environment, the body or our thoughts.

In "What Deepak Chopra told me about stress, anxiety, and happiness" (2018, Mar 16) Katie Becker helps us understand in what ways we connect stress and disease. Becker and Chopra explained mind-body connection; what happens if you do not relieve stress, and how to release it. How do you stay calm while facing the stress? Mr. Chopra answers, "You learn to manage stress, just as you learn to ride a bicycle. Everything is learnable. Everybody should know how to manage their stress, but they don't," (Becker, 2018, Mar 16, para. 11). In the conversation they discuss Chopra's personal stress experience and his view on global stress.

Dragana invites you to explore the meditative practice mentioned in the last article. When meditating, you focus on an object. To gain a deep state of peace is the aim.

Meditation is about training the mind to become calm and silent, hence you may allow deeper levels of consciousness to arise.

3) Stress or Relaxation

You either suffer from stress or relax yourself. If you are under stress, we call that a survival mode. Although this flight or fight state of being is important because it enables us to deal with dangerous situations, it is only useful for short periods of time. The part of the autonomous nervous system responsible for the stress response is a sympathetic nervous system.

Relaxation is the opposite way of functioning. We should be able to express ourselves in various ways, while maintaining a relaxed state of being. Releasing tension and anxiety ought to be a part of your daily routine.

Relief from work, effort, and various obligations is important. Is neglecting refreshing the body and mind familiar to you? Mental repose and physical unwinding might enhance your level of functioning.

The relaxation response activates the part of the autonomic nervous system called a parasympathetic nervous system.

Let's mention certain benefits of relaxation:

1. Strengthen the immune system
2. Relief of pain to an extent that varies
3. Enhanced respiratory function
4. Lowered blood pressure and cholesterol levels
5. Reduced anxiety and depression
6. Improved attention spam
7. Better sleep
8. Improved cognitive functioning

Is it important to include relaxation techniques in your busy schedule?

In our modern world we might experience prolonged periods of stress. What used to be a short-term reaction to a dangerous event in the past may even turn into a permanent condition of contemporary life. Would you agree people perform better under stress? That approach may justify the lack of relaxation. However, underestimated relaxation may have adverse effects on your health and well-being.

What undesirable outcomes can happen if you ignore relaxation?

Let us mention several common responses to the lack of relaxation:
-Weaker immune system which means there is a higher probability to catch any aliment.
- Psychosomatic diseases where stress and emotions are influencing the illness such as high blood pressure or lower back pain.
- Mood disorders,
- Digestive problems,
- Lower level of cognitive functioning.

How to overcome long term stress? Include relaxation exercises in your busy schedule!

- Make a list of relaxation techniques you find. Are you comfortable with relaxation practices? Make sure you have at least several relaxation exercises which do not require special conditions or extra resources.

-Remember beneficial effects of relaxation. Read books, attend seminars and talk with your friends about relaxation effects. In addition, you may hire the relaxation couch Dragana.

-What about conscious breathing, hypnosis or walking for 15 to 20 minutes? You may enjoy coloring books, autogenic training or conversations with supportive people. Some men, women and children also love pets and find them relaxing.

-Create relaxation habits. Take care to include the relaxation practices of your choice in your daily schedule. If you find this approach challenging, find an accountability partner and/or a relaxation coach such as the author of this book.

-Discover deeper patterns that may block your relaxation advancement. What is in your way? Maybe you need to deal with obstacles that prevent your relaxation practices.

4) About My Client Jane's Story

When I work with my coaching clients as the relaxation coach, I offer them three main routes:

First, we focus on gaining knowledge. What is stress and its effects? Then, we consider relaxation and its advantageous effects.

Second, I offer my clients the support system to include relaxation techniques in their busy schedule. Creating and maintaining relaxation habits is important, too. Sometimes, the challenge is the right choice of relaxation techniques. Or are you not sure how to customize the chosen one? For others, being consistent with their relaxation exercises is the main problem.

Third, we may explore deeper patterns that may block your relaxation advancement. We focus on factors that provoke stressful reactions.

What is in your way, what bothers you or annoys you? It may be something crucial. Sometimes, minor tasks and unpleasant situations you consider irrelevant may build up a major stressor.

The third option: what is missing in your life? Is the lack of valuable quality another stressor in your life?

Jane's Story

Here is a story of one of my clients. We'll call her Jane as she cherishes her privacy.

Jane tried several meditation techniques, but could not be persistant with them, "As if something doomed her not to relax." Jane was also interested in discovering other relaxation practices.

She explored the third option with me: the major stressors in her life. She realized that the family and the household are her oasis of peace. Her career was one of her strengths, too. So, what was the problem?

Jane created a journal of her daily stressors. The task was easy: write anything that contributes to your feelings of tension, irritation or worry. After a while, the stressor showed up. Her professional activities satisfied her, but after the engagement Jane did not go straight to her home and family. She used to spend time with people she did not get along well with and undertook activities she considered meaningless which only made her more tired.

For months, Jane could not change those "minor factors". We examined other issues like:
- Her right to say no,
- Is a change acceptable?
- Self-care
- Self-protection
- Priorities in life

We may have special qualities and accomplishments, but the fact is that we are also "ordinary humans". Remind yourself that each human being has limited time, energy, and focus at their disposal.

Later, Jane created a new schedule which allowed her to focus on her private and professional aims.

Only after that were we ready to focus on relaxation techniques. Jane explored various relaxation practices. Her favorite relaxation exercises are coloring books, playing with her pats and listening to hypnosis audio files.

It is important to notice the practices are available to all of us. They do not require special circumstances or hours of dedication. You can incorporate them into your daily obligations.

I encourage you to contemplate on the benefits of relaxation. It is possible to find relaxation techniques for you. Be persistent with your relaxation practices. Ask for help, engage with friends who appreciate relaxation and/or hire Dragana as your relaxation coach.

5) Summary of Three Online Articles on Relaxation

In this chapter we will consider benefits of relaxation. It might be necessary to study relaxation and examine your approach to it. Do you appreciate changing your thinking patterns?

Next, we contemplate whether relaxation is beneficial for people with stress-triggered medical conditions. To personalize or not your choice of the relaxation techniques, that is another question.
Last, we'll mention the effects of visualization or guided imagery.

In his article "Relaxation: surprising benefits detected" (1986, May 13) Daniel Goleman outlines benefits of relaxation, including relief for asthmatics and diabetics. Professor Goleman identifies two types of relaxation practice. First, if you enjoy gardening or catnaps, Goleman clarifies that he does not consider them relaxation.

Second, the intense relaxation allows you to change your thinking patterns and decrease the arousal of your sympathetic nervous system. The sympathetic nervous system governs the stress response. Professor Goleman observes that the intense and regular relaxation training provokes a physiological change which may be beneficial to various degrees.

According to Matthew Thorpe in "12 Science-Based Benefits of Meditation" (2017, July 5) stress reduction is the number one advantage of the relaxation technique. Doctor Thorpe explains the stress increases our level of cortisol. He relates this stress hormone to the inflammatory promoting chemicals which may cause or contribute to disrupted sleep, higher levels of anxiety and depression or unclear reasoning. Doctor Thorpe describes desirable effects of meditation as one of the popular forms of relaxation. "Many styles of meditation can help reduce stress. Meditation can also reduce symptoms in people with stress-triggered medical conditions." (Thorpe, 2017, July 5, para. 14). Thorpe explains various benefits of meditation such as anxiety reduction, enhanced self-awareness and better attention span.

In "Relaxation Techniques"(2018, Nov) Lawrence Robinson, Robert Segal, Jeanne Segal and Melinda Smith help us understand various aspects of relaxation. They describe the fight or flight response and the relaxation response. "In addition to its calming physical effects, the relaxation response also increases energy and focus, combats illness, relieves aches and pains, heightens problem-solving abilities, and boosts motivation and productivity." (Robinson et al., 2018, Nov, para. 5). The authors tell us to personalize the choice of relaxation practice and explain several relaxation exercises. Robinson et al. recommend visualization or guided imagery as a simple practice to let go of the habitual perception of the world.

6) Coloring Books and Relaxation

In this chapter we will explore coloring books as a relaxation tool. There are many people who enjoy coloring books year after year. They have favorite authors and themes. Others "colorists" prefer to discover new designers from time to time. What do they have in common? The fans appreciate the relaxing feature of the coloring books.

Let us contemplate about probable mechanisms for such an effect: -Are you verbally oriented? Images activate another side of the personality. Our "visual self" may trigger happy memories from the past.

-The coloring books allow you to enter the daydreaming state. To gain a wider perspective may have a relaxing effect. If you can distant yourself from the task, and remove your attention from established thinking patterns, peacefulness is easier to achieve. In addition, the wider perspective may improve your analysis and decision making.

-Third, for those who feel fear about the future or sadness and hopelessness for the past events, coloring books are one of the relaxation techniques of choice. Instead of focusing on the unsettling thoughts about the past or future, you may focus on the coloring book here and now. That focus on the present moment and easy coloring activity allows you to separate yourself from the distracting thought process.

-Some people/colorists are fond of a certain coloring books. Whether it is nature, fantasy, cities, human beings or something else, you are in control. The chosen theme of the coloring book gives you a chance to connect with your favorite environment, individuals or qualities. It is easy to move away from the annoying content and recharge your batteries fast.

-Coloring books are affordable and available. You can purchase them and get them ready anytime you desire. There are no extra conditions, permissions, long hours or risky environment involved. Do it; you are in control.

-Sometimes people enjoy coloring in company. The coloring with adults may deepen your level of calmness. The mutual support adds to your relaxation.

-Focus on one thing at a time with your coloring experience. Recurring simple movements allow you to unwind, too. Avoid facing many distractions you're not even interested in.

-For those involved in work or communication via electronic devices, leaving the virtual world for a while may be helpful. Coloring books are tactile. Therefore, they contribute to your relaxation.

Why to relax with Coloring Books

It seems like there are many good reasons to use coloring books. You may choose your why from activating the visual self to removing your attention away from the established reasoning patterns. Maybe your way is focusing on here and now, using easy coloring tasks. Because many coloring themes are at your disposal, you may choose the qualities, people, or space you love to color.

To appreciate coloring books is easy. They are affordable and available. Next, you are in control with coloring books. To color in company or alone, the choice is yours or it is up to you.

Next, coloring books also help you escape the virtual world for a while because they are tactile. The coloring helps you gain a wider perspective, too.

Finally, if you search for a good "why" to color and relax, you may find your why easily. Remember to personalize the coloring experience, too.

7) Summary of Three Online Articles on Relaxing Aspects of Coloring Books

Now, we are ready to check whether the coloring is art therapy. If not, what about the advantages of coloring such as simple tasks, provided guidance and predictable outcomes?

Moreover, consider the history of coloring. Not only is the coloring affordable, but also versatile activity. From time to time, we my acknowledge the other relaxation exercises, too.

Last, we'll contemplate variations regarding coloring: to color in company or alone, during the lunch breaks at work or after the busy day, for entertainment or self-care.

Dana Dovey, in her article "The Therapeutic Science of Adult Coloring Books: How This Childhood Pastime Helps Adults Relieve Stress" (2015, Oct 8) explores if coloring books are art therapy. She estimates the coloring books as an easy tool for those not confident in their artistic expression. The simple act of coloring between the lines is enough. According to Dovey's perspective, art therapists may disregard the coloring books as an art therapy technique because of its simplicity and the provided drawn guidance. In conclusion, Dovey appreciates repetitions and predictable outcomes for their calming effect on the "colorists".

As stated in "Does Coloring Really Reduce Stress?" (2016, Jan 1) people are interested in coloring for a long time. From Carl Jung's perspective on coloring mandalas to modern science, what do people find appealing to the coloring? This article explores the benefits and limitations of coloring books. "Stress is dangerous and can lead to serious health concerns. There are many methods of stress relief— coloring may be a good option for you as part of an overall approach to reducing your anxiety," (Anaheim Regional Medical Center, 2016, Jan 1, para. 9). The coloring books are popular. The article confirms the "colorists" have an affordable tool for relaxation.

Kim Painter, Specialist for the USA today, interviewed several experts in "Adult coloring books promise stress relief" (2015, Dec 13). The experts expressed their perspective on the advantages and disadvantages of coloring books. Painter comments that people use coloring books in various ways. Stress relief is not the only reason people appreciate coloring. As reported by Painter, people use coloring books in various ways. "The American Art Therapy Association has put out an official statement saying it supports the use of coloring books for 'pleasure and self-care' but hopes coloring won't take the place of therapy for those who could benefit," (Painter, 2015, December 13, para. 12). Painter contemplates professionals doing coloring books during lunch breaks. The coloring style is different; people may prefer to do it alone or with colleagues. Painter suggests both groups claim the coloring helps them relax.

8) Conclusion

What is a balanced view on relaxation and coloring books?

First, coloring books are one of the relaxation techniques. The coloring is not the one and only relaxation practice or the ultimate calming technique.

Second, the coloring is not art therapy. The missing piece is a connection to the art therapist. Besides, the techniques are less important than the therapist in the art therapy. Consider art therapy is not suitable for everyone. We may enjoy the coloring without the art therapist.

Third, coloring is not the solution for all problems. The coloring books are not panacea, but a relaxation technique of choice for people who are rather healthy and independent. For others, besides the coloring, they could inquire about the help they need.

Fourth, do not use the coloring as a replacement for other important life areas. It is not the either-or perspective: either the coloring or the lifelong learning, either the personal transformation or the coloring, either the coloring books or variety of relaxation techniques. It is up to you to use various relaxation techniques and activate other important life areas.

Now, we are clear about limitations in relation to coloring books, so we may appreciate their benefits.

Summary

In this short-read Dragana Dj. Jeremic focused on the relaxation aspects of the coloring books.

We mentioned that long-term stress has many adverse effects. The response of stress may increase your chances to become ill, sensitive to pain, weaken your cognitive functioning and mood regulation.

Therefore, conscious practice of relaxation is necessary in the contemporary world. If you would like to hire a relaxation coach, email the author of this books Dragana Dj. Jeremic at dragana@relax8.space.

Let's mention several benefits of relaxation: stronger immune system, lower blood tension, better cognitive functioning and stable moods.

One of the popular relaxation exercises is coloring. It depends on your personality and life circumstances how to use the coloring books. We may consider them available and affordable.

The coloring allows you to withdraw from the upsetting thoughts regarding past or future and focus on the present moment. It is such a relief to concentrate on one task of your choice and repeat simple movements. Anyone can color between the lines of the chosen drawings. You may color alone or with respectful adults. One way or the other the images will activate your "visual self". In addition, people involved in virtual reality acknowledge the balancing effect of coloring books. They appreciate the tactile feature of the coloring. As a result, it is easy to celebrate the present moment with coloring books.

References

Becker, K. (2018, March 16). What Deepak Chopra told me about stress, anxiety, and happiness. *Coveteur*. Retrieved May 25, 2019, from http://coveteur.com/2018/03/16/deepak-chopra-stress-anxiety-happiness-wisdom/

Do I need to have an art background to color? (n. d.). *Art Therapy Coloring*. Retrieved May 25, 2019, from https://arttherapycoloring.com/do-adult-coloring-books-require-experience/

Does Coloring Really Reduce Stress? (2016, January 30). *Anaheim Regional Medical Center*. Retrieved May 25, 2019, from https://www.anaheimregionalmc.com/Blog/2016/January/Does-Coloring-Really-Reduce-Stress-.aspx

Dovey, D. (2015, October 8). The Therapeutic Science of Adult Coloring Books: How This Childhood Pastime Helps Adults Relieve Stress. *Medical Daily*. Retrieved May 25, 2019, from https://www.medicaldaily.com/therapeutic-science-adult-coloring-books-how-childhood-pastime-helps-adults-356280

Goleman, D. (1986, May 13). Relaxation: surprising benefits detected. *The New York Times*. Retrieved May 25, 2019, from https://www.nytimes.com/1986/05/13/science/relaxation-surprising-benefits-detected.html

Painter, K. (2015, December 13). Adult coloring books promise stress relief. *USA Today*. Retrieved May 25, 2019, from https://www.usatoday.com/story/life/2015/12/13/adult-coloring-books-stress/76916842/

Robinson, L., Segal, R., Segal, J., & Smith, M. (2018, November). Relaxation Techniques. *Help guide*. Retrieved May 25, 2019, from https://www.helpguide.org/articles/stress/relaxation-techniques-for-stress-relief.htm

Scott, E. (2018, October 30). Understanding and managing stressors. *Very Well Mind*. Retrieved May 25, 2019, from https://www.verywellmind.com/what-are-stressors-3145149

The effects of stress on your body.(2017, December 10). *Web MD.*
Retrieved May 21, 2019, from
https://www.webmd.com/balance/stress-
management/effects-of-stress-on-your-body

Thorpe, M. (2017, July 5). 12 Science-Based Benefits of
Meditation. *Health line.* Retrieved May 21, 2019, from
https://www.healthline.com/nutrition/12-benefits of-
meditation

Also, by Dragana Dj. Jeremic on Amazon

Pawsome Friends: A Community Book Project

The book is created by Donna Kozik and 100+ contributing authors in 2019. As one of the contributing authors Dragana DJ. Jeremic wrote a short essay and a quote on the pet.

Dragana's Five Fantasy Coloring books

Dragana DJ. Jeremic is glad to inform you about her new fantasy coloring system named DETERMINED coloring book which was created in 2019.

Firstly, we have several perspectives. Secondly, Dragana presents each perspective on three levels based on the number and size of the main elements, here cherry blossoms. We may compare it to an establishing shot, American shot and close up in the film industry. Thirdly, Dragana adds the imaginary elements to each level: fantasy, symbol and. mandala patterns in natural environment.

In 2024, Dragana wrote her books and participated in another community project imagined by Donna Kozik.

Hats Off to Quantum-Touch

Becoming HeartMath Practitioner

HeartMath Affinity 1

HeartMath Affinity 2, Simple Techniques

HeartMath Affinity 3: Freeze Frame Technique

HeartMath Materialization, Hardcover

Dragana listened to readers who appreciated her three short-read books: HeartMath Affinity 1,2, 3 and requested them in one book. Additionally, you are going to find Bonus 1,2 and 3. Surprise!
This book gives the response to a popular question: Could that HeartMath certification of yours be helpful with goal achievement?

The cover photograph is shot by Dragana Dj. Jeremic and it displays University of Belgrade Faculty of Laws' edifice which was built in 1937. The organization has been one of the oldest educational institutions not only in Belgrade, but also in the region. It was established in 1808, so we may contemplate the influence and contribution numerous jurists have made so far.

https://en.wikipedia.org/wiki/University_of_Belgrade_Faculty_of_Law

Memoirs: HeartMath and QT, Hardcover

Dragana listened to readers who appreciated her two short-read books on Amazon: Becoming HeartMath Practitioner and Hats Off to Quantum-Touch and requested them in one book. She added the third part as well as Bonus 1, 2 and 3. Surprise! We are going to explore Quantum-Touch healing circles, too.

Celebrating 365 Days of Gratitude

Dragana participated for the second time in the Community book project organized by Donna Kozik in 2024. The content is presented in months hence you may find Dragana's contribution on July 20. It is titled Meditation and Action.

Relaxation and Coloring, Hardcover

In this hardcover book, we appreciate Dragana's two books which were previously published on Amazon:
Stress, Relaxation and Coloring Books & Fantasy Cherry Blossoms as well as Bonus 1 and 2. Sounds great!
Therefore, we may appreciate short and simple techniques while waiting for the tram or bus and color more complex coloring books in the privacy of our homes or with friends.

SoundCloud/CoachDragana

You may find compelling stories there as well as lovely musicians at https://SoundCloud.com

Then you may search for Coach Dragana.

Stream CoachDragana music | Listen to songs, albums, playlists for free on SoundCloud

Whereas Dragana has made some audio files dedicated to her books on Amazon, you may check others that show in what ways we are not perfect, meaning there is a variety of circumstances and options in the outer world. However, it is our duty to choose wisely and navigate well those best options for the time being which we have chosen well.

www.ingramcontent.com/pod-product-compliance
Lightning Source LLC
Chambersburg PA
CBHW070343290526
45791CB00003B/1446